Zen-Sational Basketball Shooting

(Using Your Mind and Body Together to Reach Your Potential as a Shooter)

By David Ranney
1208 Newton Street
Bellingham, WA 98229
david@innerbasketball.com
www.pureperformancesports.com
www.innerbasketball.com
www.innerbaseball.com
www.maxtennis.com

Zen-Sational Basketball Shooting

Published by:
Night Lotus Books
1208 Newton St
Bellingham, Wash. 98229

Printed in the United States

ISBN-13: 978-1477518465

ISBN-10: 1477518460

Zen-Sational Basketball Shooting

Contents

An Introduction To The Mental Game 7

About David Ranney 9

How to Make These Lessons Work for You 13

What You Will Learn When You Read These Lessons
....15

Your Psychic Reading 16

Lesson No. 1: The Mental Game and Winning Defined
....17

    What is the Mental Game Anyway 17

    Why I Don't Want You To Try To Win & The Ultimate
    Goal...19

Lesson No. 2: How Does Judgment Interfere With Your
Play? 22

Lesson No. 3: The Core Principles of the Mental Game
....24

    The Principle of Consciousness............................24

    The Principle of Focus 25

    The Principle of Relaxation 25

    The Principle of Playing Without Judgment 25

    The Mental Game Core Principle Statements.........26

Lesson No. 4: "The Process" For Learning 28

Lesson No. 5: Some Important Things You Need To
Know About Shooting Baskets 32

Lesson No. 6: An Undervalued Technique: Holding the
Follow Through..34

Zen-Sational Basketball Shooting

Lesson No. 7: Shooting on the UpForce 35

Lesson No. 8: Focus On the Hook? What's That? 37

Lesson No. 9: Breathing: An Unknown But Powerful
Technique 39

Lesson No. 10: Relaxation: Why It Works & How To Do
It 42

Lesson No. 11: Make More Free Throws. Guaranteed!
.... 45

    The Full Visualization Technique 46

    Things You Need To Stop Doing when Shooting
    Free Throws 47

    The Quick Visualization Technique 48

Lesson No. 12: When Shooting Free Throws In Front
Of Crowds (Friendly or Hostile) Bother You 48

Lesson No. 13: When You Miss a Shot 51

Lesson No. 14: Some Powerful Statements 53

Lesson No. 15: Why Choke When You Don't Have To
.... 54

Lesson No. 16: Six Things You Absolutely Have To
Work On When Practicing Your Shooting 57

Lesson No. 17: Keeping Unproductive or Destructive
Thoughts Away 58

Lesson No. 18: Do You Shoot Differently in Your
Warm-up Than You Do When the Game Starts? 61

Lesson No. 19: How To Decide When To Shoot 62

Lesson No. 20: Don't waste Time When You Are Sitting
On the Bench Waiting To Go Into The Game Again ... 64

Lesson No. 21: A Short Review of What To Do When You Play In Your Games 65

Lesson No. 22: Have You Done Your Foundation Work? 66

Lesson No. 23: How Well Are You Doing the Core Principles? 69

Lesson No. 24: Why Losing or Missing Shots Is Good 70

Lesson No. 25: Cause and Results: What is this all about? 72

Lesson No. 26: The Value of Playing "Big Games" or Tournaments 74

Lesson No. 27: Use These Defensive Moves 75

Lesson No. 28: How to Know If You Are Playing The Mental Game Properly 77

Lesson No. 29: How to Know If You Are Actually Improving? 79

   Danny Miles' Point System 80

   Chuck Randall's Point System 81

Lesson No. 30: What Is EFT ? 83

Lesson No. 31: Prepare Yourself Before You Play and Analyze Your Shooting After You Play 85

Lesson No. 32: What To Do When You Have A Question And Don't Know The Answer (The Wondering Technique) 92

Lesson No. 33: Does Being Complimented Or Being Congratulated Really Help You To Play Better? 94

5

Lesson No. 34: Exercises You Must Do to Improve
Your Shooting..97
Lesson No. 35: Some Final Thoughts 99

An Introduction To The Mental Game

Welcome and congratulations for taking the 1st step in mastering the mental game of shooting basketballs. You are about to learn some concepts and techniques that will absolutely improve your shooting big time. That is if you read these lessons and then work on the ideas and skills presented here.

OK, it may take some time and nothing substitutes for shooting lots of basketballs, but you will learn faster and achieve a higher level of skill than using the traditional methods only.

As you may know, I do not get into a great deal of the actual mechanics of how to shoot. There are other great coaches out there that can teach you that. I will, however, give you some resources so that if you want to learn some "killer" approaches on how to shoot, you can explore them on your own. Here I will be giving you mostly mental concepts and techniques only.

I also want you to know what you can do to "fix" things when you start missing too many shots. You want to be able to do this right now and not wait for the next game or the next 5 games to get back "your groove."

I am also assuming that what you are doing now isn't working so well and you are searching for a better way. Am I right?

Are you ready to change? Are you ready to remake the way you shoot a basketball and become a phenomenally shooter? If you will do the things you read here, you will have to improve. Guaranteed. Not only will your shooting improve but, guess what, you may even enjoy playing more.

In order to really play up to your potential you must figure out how to attain the proper state of mind. This is where the "Zen stuff" comes into play. So, what is this Zen stuff all about? The word *Zen* is from the Japanese pronunciation of the Chinese word **Chán** which can be approximately translated as "meditation" or "meditative state."

No, you don't have to go to India, Japan or China and sit in a cave to learn to meditate because I will give you everything you need to do and know in this book.

Plus, these lessons will be in simple terms, they will be easy to understand, and for the most part the lessons are very short.

I know a person who is a Zen Buddhist. One day I asked him how he practiced being one. He said he did a lot of meditations and I asked him to give me an example. He said that he would just meditate and listen to all the sounds around him with no thoughts or judgments, but just being aware of them.

Well, guess what? This is what I have you do in many of my lessons, except you are being aware of what is happening not only on the basketball court but also what is going on inside of you that may be interfering with you playing your very best or what is helping you to play your very best. And, of course, this is all happening without judgments.

In order to really bring your shooting to its highest level, you must figure out how to attain a meditative state of mind. In this book, I will give you many things to focus (meditate) on and many ideas as to how you can achieve your goal of shooting the best that you are capable of.

This is a process that will never end, but I can promise you that if you will learn to shoot the way I lay out for you in this book, you will find playing the game of basketball ever so much more fun and rewarding not to mention shooting much better.

Before I get into these lessons, let me tell you a little about me and how I got started teaching the mental game and the best lesson I ever received.

About David Ranney

Although I have worked mostly with tennis players, if you think about it, many of the same mental skills of tennis can apply to shooting a basketball or just about any sport.

Let me get started by telling you my story and how I got into playing and teaching peak performance techniques.

- I started playing tennis tournaments when I was 10 years old.
- I was ranked #2 in Southern, CA in the 15 & under.
- I was ranked #2 in Southern, CA in the 18 & under.
- I was nationally ranked #6 in Singles in the 18 & under division.
- I was nationally ranked #3 in Doubles in the 18 & under division.
- I had the honor of representing the U.S. at Junior Wimbledon where I got to the semi-finals. I lost to the Russian, which was the last person I wanted to lose to. Can you guess why I maybe didn't play very well? If you don't know, you will know after reading this e-book. To give you a little hint, it was because I tried way too hard to win.
- I played on the Junior Davis Cup team.

Zen-Sational Basketball Shooting

- I played on the USC tennis team and the three years I lettered varsity we were National Champions.

As you can see I was a pretty good player, but not a great one.

But, I had a big problem. My attitude stunk and I was very negative. I used to yell and scream on the tennis court because I would get so incredibly frustrated. I thought that if I could only stroke the ball perfectly I would never miss. But of course, I couldn't do that every time, and boy did I try hard. And, my attitude was horrible.

I hated myself for getting so angry and frustrated, but I couldn't stop. I had no idea why I played badly at times, and I didn't have a clue as to how to turn my game around when I wasn't playing well. Neither did I know how to "make" myself play well.

I never beat players who were just a little better than I was. Remember I told you that I was ranked #2 in Southern California in the 15 and 18 and under. Well, a player named Jerry Cromwell was the one who was ranked #1 and I never ever beat him. I don't think anyone tried harder than I did but I just couldn't beat him.

After college, I began teaching tennis the traditional way until my conversion to teaching the Inner Game when I was in my 30s. What happened was that one day I was reading the *LA Magazine* about an instructor who was teaching the *Inner Game of Tennis*. His name was Tim Gallwey. After reading about him, I knew I had to have a lesson from this man, and I was determined to go to the ends of the earth to find him. As it turned out, he was right there in my hometown of Los Angeles.

To make a long story longer, I took two lessons from Tim, and he completely changed my life. In the first 10 minutes into the lesson, I felt that the weight of the world was taken off my back. I never got angry or yelled again – an amazing accomplishment since I had already spent all of my tennis life getting upset with myself.

It was the best lesson I ever received and it changed my life forever.

All of a sudden my tennis game was more consistent, and overnight my endurance increased. I wasn't so tense all the time, and this shift allowed me to keep my energy focused on mastering the mental game. For the first time, I was beating people I never could beat before. I was winning close matches and hitting balls that I never had been able to hit before.

My doubles partner at the time, Keith Nielson, whom I played once a week said that it wasn't as much fun to play me anymore because he couldn't get me angry.

To sum it all up, I felt like a completely new person when I was on the court.

After I took the two lessons from Tim Gallwey, he not only completely changed my own tennis game but also my whole way of teaching. I asked Tim to come to the Jack Kramer Tennis Club, where I was an assistant teaching pro under Robert Lansdorp, so he could give clinics to all of my students. There I watched Tim in action. As a result, I adapted his ideas and modified them slightly to fit my own way of teaching.

I will be forever grateful to Tim Gallwey for showing me how to make this change. His book, *The Inner Game of Tennis*, has been my "Tennis Bible" and is truly one of the best books ever written on the mental aspects of playing sports. You can find his book in most bookstores.

In the 25 plus years since then, I have been studying the mental game so that I could achieve the state of mind that would allow my body to play at its very best. I wanted to know how to play "out of my mind"

11

every time I played. The concepts I will present to you here will show you how to do this. These concepts, as you will see, are easy to talk about, but it takes practice to get there.

I knew that these ideas worked for me, but I wasn't sure if they would work for anybody else. Over the years I have worked with many beginners, average players and good tournament tennis players in addition to some varsity high school and college basketball players to know that it works and that anyone can do it.

However, it is a process and you can use them for the rest of your basketball life. I am at an age where ones game is supposed to be going "over the hill" but I am still learning new things about myself and my tennis game is actually getting better. With these concepts, you too, will see improvement as long as you play.

As to my basketball experience, it isn't very much. I did play on the Jr Varsity basketball team in high school, but in my senior year I didn't try out for the varsity team as I needed to concentrate on my tennis.

When I was living in Victoria, B.C., I started to play tennis with and coach a man named Manny Baines. Not only was he a good tennis player, but he was one of the best basketball players on Vancouver Island. As he learned the principles of the mental game of tennis, he would apply them to his basketball. Needless to say, he found them extremely powerful.

I also had another friend who had a young daughter who played high school basketball. Since I knew that the mental part that I teach in tennis applied to any sport, I worked with her a little on applying the principles specifically to basketball. Her Dad then worked with her over the years on these ideas as both of them realized how powerful the concepts are.

More recently, I have worked with some of the players on the Western Washington university men's and women's varsity team.

How to Make These Lessons Work for You

To maximize the benefits of this book, first familiarize yourself with, and if possible, memorize the Mental Game Core Principles (Lesson No. 3). These principles will give you the foundation for every tip, idea, and instruction in this book. I suggest that you keep a copy of these Core Principles with you so that you can read them every time before you play. **Using these Core Principles is an absolute must for when you play.**

The Lessons in this book are listed in a deliberate order. Even though these lessons are in order of how I believe you should learn them, I would like to encourage you to read through the entire book first.

Reading through the entire book first is extremely important because there are so many important lessons that you will want to know right now. It is also the only way for you to know everything there is to know about playing the Mental Game and give you an idea as to what is in store for you as you go back and work on the lessons one at a time.

Then go back and start with Lesson No. 1. and read and work with one lesson at a time spending as much time on each lesson for as long as you like until you feel the need to move on.

However, you have my permission to skip to any lesson at any time if you are having a particular problem. Aren't you glad I gave you permission? ☺

Zen-Sational Basketball Shooting

Even though you are working through each lesson one at a time, I would suggest that you re-read the entire book again after 3 months, 6 months, 9 months, and then after 1 year. After 1 year, you should have been able to work through all the lessons. Then I would suggest that you re-read the book once a year.

As you'll see throughout this book, I have bolded some words, phrases, or sentences. Please pay particular attention to these words as they will be critical to your improvement.

All this being said, you may approach using these lessons any way that feels right for you. The only really important thing is that you read the lessons, implement them into your play and keep working on your Mental Game for as long as you continue playing basketball.

I would suggest that you put this book on your Kindle, Nook, or iPad and that you keep it with you so that you can refer to it at anytime.

It would be good to read the lesson you want to work on at home and then again just before you get on the court. That way you will really know and understand the lessons you are working on when you go to play.

In order to really make these lessons work, you must have them pretty much memorized. You can't say to your coach, team or your opponent, "Hold on a minute while I look at the lesson on ….."

There is another thing that you will find when you read through the lessons. I will be repeating myself over and over and over again about the three main concepts that absolutely must be worked on in order to make everything work.

These are seeing the hook, breathing, and relaxing. Please don't get tired of hearing me talk about them. It has been my experience that
14

most of my students do not take these things as seriously as they really are, as they must be done every time you play – and on every shot you take in order to play the way you want.

These students finally "get it" after constant reminders, and when they do they see how much better they shoot. I am hoping that you are not one of these and that you not only get it the first time, but are actually able to put these concepts into practice immediately.

What You Will Learn When You Read These Lessons

These series of lessons will spell out very precisely what playing the Mental Game looks like and how you will know if you are doing it right. You are going to learn some very helpful concepts about how to practice your shooting and the Mental Game that you won't find anywhere else. These concepts are the result of over 25 years of studying, practicing, and teaching the inner game.

After you read these lessons one by one and put these principles into play, you will be entering a whole different way of shooting that will speed up your learning and help you enjoy the game more.

However, there is a catch. You still have to read each lesson more than once. You also will have to be willing to change the way you think and allow yourself to believe in shooting this way. You have to practice it and truly use it. If you only read the lessons, you will not get the improvements you want. You have to apply these techniques as soon as you learn and understand them.

In this book, I won't get into the whole philosophy behind the Mental Game. You can get this information from reading Timothy Gallwey's *The Inner Game of Tennis*. In fact, Gallwey's book is really required reading, as it will give you the background to what I am trying to teach you. In my opinion, the other present-day books on sports psychology pretty much rehash what Tim Gallwey wrote over 30 years ago, only not as eloquently. Yeah, I know his book is about tennis, but please trust me when I tell you that it is an absolute must for you to read no matter what sport you are playing.

The mental part always comes first and mastering the mental part of the game so you can play in the zone remains the ultimate goal. However, you also need to work on your mechanics and do the drills, in addition to the mental side.

Your Psychic Reading

Did you know I am also a psychic? Well, I am and I am going to give you a reading right now concerning your basketball shooting.

I am now looking into my crystal ball which will tell all about your basketball game. Just give me a few seconds to get into my trance. Omm-m-m.

I see that you love the game of basketball, but you feel that you are just not shooting the best you can. At times (maybe most of the time), you are not enjoying yourself because you are getting more and more frustrated and you just don't know why you are missing so many shots. You are trying so hard to shoot correctly, trying so hard to play well, and trying so hard to win, and you just can't seem to

16

make it happen. You want more from basketball, and so you are searching for a different or better way of shooting.

So, how did I do? Do you now believe I am psychic? Please check your mailbox in a couple of days for my $125 invoice for this reading.

In the next part, I will talk about how the principles I learned in tennis apply to basketball to help you shoot much much better. Guaranteed.

Lesson No. 1: The Mental Game and Winning Defined

Before I get into the actual techniques, I need you to understand exactly what the mental game really is and how thinking (or not thinking) about winning fits into the picture.

So you will get two Lessons here. One on the mental game and one about winning. Please be sure to read both.

What is the Mental Game Anyway

The first order of business is to know what the mental game really is. Most people just don't know what it is or how to work on it so to get started I have three questions that you need to ask yourself. Don't worry if you can't answer all the questions correctly. By the time you finish reading this, you will know all.

- What % of the game do you think is mental?
- What % of the time that you play and practice do you work on your mental game?
- If you were going to work on your mental game, what is it and how would you work on it?

Most people say that the mental game is anywhere from 75 to 100% and most people answer that even though they feel that the game is this percentage, they don't practice it anywhere close to it if at all.

On the last question, most people don't have a clue or they give me some vague answer about what the mental game is. This last one is the really important one because if you don't know what the mental game is, how can you even begin to practice it.

Here is my definition of the mental game:

The mental game is the relationship between your "conscious mind," your "other than conscious mind," and your body. It is your "conscious mind" which sets the goals then it gets out of the way and lets the "other than conscious mind" direct the body, which then shoots the ball. The strength, direction, and quality of your outer skills are determined by this inner relationship. When you pursue and find this ideal mental state, you will be shooting and playing your very best.

An example is to be found when you think about how you drive a car. Your conscious mind has a huge purpose as it has to see where you are going so that you don't hit any other cars, people, bicycles, etc. It also has to see where the road goes and needs to read the road signs if you need to find a particular street. However, when you steer the car, hopefully you don't think about how you move the steering wheel and I know you don't think about how your foot presses the gas pedal or the brake pedal. You just do it.

18

Well, playing basketball, or any sport, is no different. It is just more complicated. Because we have been taught that we must control our bodies so that we can shoot the ball into the basket, you may not have even thought about just letting your body function without conscious control.

Your conscious mind has a role to play but you need to learn how to get the part that will interfere out of the way when it comes to actually shooting. Please believe me when I tell you, your body is what shoots the ball and it knows far better how to do this than the conscious mind telling it how.

As a natural by-product, you will find that your enjoyment of your playing will be enhanced. This is because you will be calmer and more relaxed, and of course, you will be shooting better.

Why I Don't Want You To Try To Win & The Ultimate Goal

Do you think that winning is the ultimate goal? I hope not and if you do, I am hoping to change your mind. In the mean time, would you like to learn how your team can win every time it played?

If winning is your ultimate goal, then I have a deal for you. If I can tell you how your team can win every time it plays, and I can, do you think your team would pay me $10,000? No? OK, maybe winning isn't that important so how about paying me only $1,000? Well, you can save your money because I will tell you how your team can win every time anyway, and for free.

In order to win every time, you just need to play a team with two year olds on it. If you can't beat that team every time, then you are in

19

really big trouble. You do know why you would win every time, right?

Maybe now you can begin to see that winning may not be a goal that will bring you the most satisfaction or pleasure even though winning can be a lot of fun and profitable if you are on a school or professional team. Before we talk more about what I believe is a better ultimate goal, let's talk a little more about winning.

I have another trick question for you and let's see if you can get the answer. I can tell you who has won every game that has ever been played, and I can tell you who will win every game that will be played in the future.

How can I make this statement?

Here is the answer: The team who plays better on that given day will be the winner. So, if your team plays better than your opponent today, you will win. Did you get the answer right?

The point of this is that winning will take care of itself, and if your team strives and learns to play at the top of their game and that "top" is better than your opponent, guess what, your team will automatically win. And if your team plays twice as well as it ever had but still loses the game, most likely your team will probably feel pretty good knowing that they played very well.

On an individual level, if you don't like how well you played, then you need to figure out how you can play better in the future. This means that you will need to practice more of both the physical and the mental game.

So, how do you play at the top of your game? You will play your best by using the concepts I will teach you in this book. Another way to say it is to spend more and more time figuring out how to get your conscious mind out of the way so your body can play its very best. You will also find that when you practice these concepts, your body will learn faster and more easily. I can't describe to you what this state of being feels like, but I can guide you so that you can begin to discover for yourself what it feels like and how to get there.

Let's get back to the ultimate goal.

I believe the ultimate goal is for you to find out how to play your very best every time you play.

This goal not only helps your team accomplish the other goal of winning but winning will happen automatically and without you thinking about it.

- **Thinking about winning when you are playing in a tight game is DEATH and will not lead you very often to shooting your best.**
- **Trying hard to win will not always lead you to shooting your best.**
- **Trying to not lose doesn't work that well either.**

How many times have you seen your team or another team blow it in the last few minutes of a game? I don't think the team blew it because they weren't trying hard to win. I believe it is because they were focusing on winning instead of focusing on the things that they needed to do to play well enough to win. I see this happen all the time.

Most of you know who John Wooden is. Some people say he is the greatest athletic coach ever and not just the greatest basketball coach. Do you know how often he talked about winning to his players? If you guessed never, then you would be correct. So, there must be a good reason why the greatest coach ever, never ever talked about winning and he didn't want his players thinking about winning either.

Do you know why thinking about winning is not productive? Do you know how it affects your body? Thinking leads to trying which leads to tension which may lead to not shooting very well. **Thinking about and doing what you need to do to shoot your very best is by far better and will lead to helping your team to win more games.**

As I said earlier, the path to this state of being can be found in the Mental Game Core Principles. Mastering these Core Principles will be a lifelong process. You will be discovering things about yourself and your game for the rest of your basketball life. And who knows, maybe you will find some of these principles useful in other areas of your life as well.

Lesson No. 2: How Does Judgment Interfere With Your Play?

I have already talked to you about the mental game, what it is and about winning. Now you have another issue that must be addressed if you are going to be able to continue your journey on this path of getting the most from your body.

So, if you are going to be playing the mental game, there is one huge issue that if you don't or can't deal with, then this way of playing I am going to teach you will not work for you.

This issue is how you deal with "judgment."

Zen-Sational Basketball Shooting

If you like to judge yourself, your shooting, and/or how well you are doing etc, you will need to change your thoughts as they will interfere with you shooting your best.

One of the most important concepts is letting go of judgments. I am not saying not to be aware of what is going on and what is working and not working. I mean judgments as to whether you are shooting good or bad or whether you hit a three pointer or you missed the rim altogether. There are no bad shots. There are only shots that didn't go the way you wanted them to go. Likewise, there are no good shots. There are only shots that went the way you wanted them to.

When you judge your shooting, how well you are playing, or anything else, it is unproductive and can even cause you to do worse.

The natural response to your judgments is to try harder. For example, if you judge your last shot as being a bad one, what is your response? You may say to yourself, OK, I missed my last shot and from now on I will try harder to make the next one. This leads to using your conscious mind to start controlling your body, thereby becoming more tense. The same thing happens when you have made a lot of good shots or made a lot of good plays. You will try harder the next time to keep shooting good etc and your body will probably get tense leading you to making more errors. As you can see, this is a vicious circle.

Although trying harder may seem to work in the short run, you will find that when the game gets tight or when it comes time for your team to win, your individual play may break down.

The letting go of judgments is not easy, but even if you just begin to deal with them, you will begin to see things happen to your play and maybe even immediately.

Please take some time to work on your judgments. As you learn to let go of them and just let your body play relaxed, you will be on your way to playing your very best.

In the next part, I will talk about how the core principles I learned in tennis apply to shooting a basketball to help you shoot your very best. Guaranteed.

Lesson No. 3: The Core Principles of the Mental Game

The Core Principles are the foundation, backbone, and just about everything you need to play your very best. If you can do these when you play, you won't need to do anything else.

There are four primary parts to the Core Principles of the mental game: Consciousness, Focus, Relaxation, and Judgment.

The Principle of Consciousness

We all have a "conscious mind" and an "other than conscious mind". I have chosen to use "conscious mind" and "other than conscious mind" because my friend and NLP master Dave Dobson coined this phrase and it seems to me to better describe what is going on in the body.

The mental game encourages you to keep your "conscious mind" calm and clear. It will also focus on what it needs to while letting your "other than conscious mind" emerge. You can and will learn to

24

"program" this "other than conscious mind" with visualization and/or talking to yourself and I will teach you how later.

The Principle of Focus

Focus lets your "conscious mind" continually notice or pay attention to some aspect of the game. You use focus to put your attention on things like seeing the hook, proper breathing or some part of your body that you want your "other than conscious mind" to respond to.

The Principle of Relaxation

Although relaxation is the general principle, proper breathing is the most important and biggest component of it. Breathing supplies the rhythm of relaxation and this helps keep your upper body from getting tense, thereby allowing your "other than conscious mind" to use your body to its greatest potential. Relaxing other parts of your body when you do your physical actions makes up the complete principle of relaxation.

The Principle of Playing Without Judgment

As I said earlier, when you judge how well you are shooting, or anything else, it is unproductive and can even cause you to shoot worse. The natural response to your judgments is to try harder. This leads to using your "conscious mind" to start controlling your body, thereby becoming more tense. Although trying harder may seem to work in the short term, you will find that when the game gets tight or when it comes time to win, your shooting may break down. This will be especially true when you have to shoot a free throw when there are only seconds to go and you need to make them to win the game.

These Core Principles should be anchored into your "other than conscious mind." By activating these principles before you play and as needed during your playing, your "conscious mind", your "other than conscious mind", and your body will be in the best possible place to work together so that you can play at the top of your game.

The Mental Game Core Principle Statements

Remember that the idea here is to truly get the destructive parts of your "conscious mind" out of the way and turn over your play to your "other than conscious mind." The "conscious mind's" role is also to help you focus on the hook and your breathing. By programming yourself with these principles, you will be able to quickly and easily get into a proper state of mind. It just takes practice and discipline.

The following statements make up the Core Principles:

- Soon I will be able to pay attention and focus on the hook. This is Core.

- As I focus on the hook, I will keep it on the hook until the ball actually gets to the rim.

- As I become more competent in focusing on the hook, my breathing will become more natural, and I will learn to be exhaling with a sigh before shooting the ball and exhaling through and long after the ball leaves my hand. This is Core.

- I shoot the ball "knowing" where I want it to go without effort and without judgment. Without judgment means truly letting the ball go where it goes, truly accepting how well I am shooting, truly accepting how well I am seeing the hook, truly accepting how well I am breathing, and truly accepting anything else that is happening while I am playing. This is Core.

- When I am sitting on the bench and if I am missing many of my shots, I will visualize or talk to myself about shooting, using a perfect motion, **consciously** seeing the hook perfectly, **consciously** exhaling before and after shooting the ball and **consciously** seeing all my shots going into the basket. This is Core.

- My conscious mind stays calm and clear and I let my other than conscious mind direct my body to shoot the ball into the basket. This is Core.

- During foul shots or time outs, I sometimes inhale deeply and exhale slowly with a sigh to relax myself and clear my mind. This is Core.

- My shooting motions are smooth and relaxed through the entire motion and my arm comes to a perfect stop until the ball gets to the rim. This is Core.

- When sitting on the bench, I clear my mind, relax my body and, if necessary, reprogram my "other than conscious mind" to do any of the above. This is Core.

- My other than conscious mind communicates to me any changes to be made. If I am missing my shots and I don't know why, I will use the "wondering technique" This is Core.

- In doing all of the above I am letting my "other than conscious mind" figure out how to make it happen, rather than trying to force myself to do anything by using my conscious mind. This is Core.

Lesson No. 4: "The Process" For Learning

In the last lesson, I gave you the core principles. As I said they are absolutely necessary for you to know so I hope you have begun to read them before every game and are working on them.

This lesson is also a very critical one because every time you want to work on learning anything and not just basketball stuff but anything, this technique is the absolute best way to learn.

However, like anything worthwhile it needs to be studied and practiced. You will want to use this technique in many of my lessons. You can certainly use it if you need to make a change in your shooting or if you are learning a new move. It works big time.

OK, it may not help you learn a new move overnight but it will shorten the learning curve immensely. Please learn this technique and then use it.

Remember, this process can be used for working on, changing, or learning any new physical movements or mental behaviors. I decided to give it to you here in the general form so that you can apply it not only to basketball but to any other activity that you are learning.

For some reason, this process is really difficult for many to remember how to do it. Maybe it is because I use it for so many different issues and it doesn't seem like it is the same process.

Please please learn it backwards and forewords so that you can use it effectively. It is probably the most powerful technique on the planet for learning.

Reminder: If you are applying this process to your basketball shooting and if you are able to, still keep focusing on the hook and/or your breathing while doing the process below. It will be more valuable to you but it is not critical. The important thing is no matter what area of life you are working on, keep relaxing and letting your body and/or mind learn.

Step 1: The Goal

This goal must be very specific and you need to know exactly and in detail what you want to accomplish. This means that you may need the services of a professional if you are not clear as to how to do whatever it is that you want to learn.

Step 2: Dry run practice and/or visualize

If you are working on a physical one, you must actually do it using a practice movement (shadow movements) before using it in the actual play. If you can't do this practice movement correctly in real speed, then do it in slow motion building up to full speed. You should also visualize and/or feel the movement you are working on. This visualization and practice movement must be absolutely correct in every way. Have your coach watch you to make sure you are getting it correct.

If you are working on a mental goal, you will only be able to visualize or talk to yourself accomplishing this goal. Again, you must visualize this goal perfectly and in every detail.

Step 3: Live practice

If you are working on a physical movement, you will just feel and be aware of what is happening in your body without a lot of trying hard to make it happen as you do whatever activity you are working on.

Without a lot of trying is another way of saying that you want to be doing the movement with a lot of relaxation. This is critical. The biggest mistake people make after they visualize something is they then try hard to make it happen. Please guard against doing this.

If you are working on a mental one, you will need to be aware of your mental processes to determine if your goal is happening.

30

Step 4: Comparing your goal with the live practice

If you are working on a physical movement and as you are being aware and feeling your body and what it is doing, you will need to now compare what you are actually doing with your ideal goal.

If your body is not learning and you are not making progress toward your goal, then you will need to go back to Step 2. Once you get to Step 3 again you must relax some part of your body more and/or stop trying so hard as the tension and trying is preventing your body from executing the physical movement the way you want it to. Pretty soon, as you relax properly, this new physical movement will begin to happen automatically and when you are not thinking about it.

If you are working on a mental concept or behavior, then be aware of your thoughts. Again, if the thoughts are not in accordance with your goal, then re-program your thought pattern and go back to Step 2.

You will do this process over and over again until it begins to happen automatically.

Let's move on and talk about how all this "mental stuff" relates to shooting a basketball. I will start out by discussing what you need to know and to focus on.

Lesson No. 5: Some Important Things You Need To Know About Shooting Baskets

Before you shoot any balls, there are some general but important things you need to know. Obviously, you need to know where the basket is. You need to know the distance to the basket as well as the trajectory you want your ball to follow. You also will need to know what mental and physical state you want to be in so that you can make the highest percentage of baskets. Let's discuss how to handle these in order.

In order to know where the basket is, you need to see it. Duh! This means that before or as you shoot, you need to be focused on the hook. You will learn all about "the hook" in Lesson No. 8. And, before you even get on the court, you need to know that when you are focusing on the hook, you want the ball to pass just over the rim and into the basket.

If you have not "spelled" this information out formally to your "other than conscious mind", you need to spend some time imagining and/or visualizing this. This 'spelling out" needs to be done continuously especially if your shooting is "off". It is not just a onetime thing.

Then you need to know the distance. How can you know this exactly enough in order to have the ball go the right distance? First of all, your conscious mind does not know the exact distance, but it does know the general distance. This one is a short one. This shot is a long one, but it doesn't know the exact distance and how to make the ball go that exact distance. However, your "other than conscious mind"

32

does know and if it doesn't it will learn very quickly when and if given the chance.

The way your body, which is to say your "other than conscious mind", will learn is through feedback. If your ball goes too short, you will need to re-program your body to have the ball go farther the next time you shoot from that distance. Likewise, if your ball went too far, you will have to re-program your body to shoot a little easier.

By the way, easier is a code word for being more relaxed. Likewise, if your shot went off to the right or left, you will need to re-program your body to shoot in the right direction. You do this by imagining and visualizing the ball going perfectly into the basket, then letting go and not trying to make it happen. You may want to take a number of shots from the same position on the court so that your "other than conscious mind" can really learn what it needs to know.

The last thing you will need to know is what the ideal arc or trajectory will be for your ball. Speaking of the arc, do you know what the proper arc is? When I see just about all players shoot, including the pros, I see a way too flat of an arc. When you look at the best shooters, you will see them shoot at a much higher arc.

OK, what is the proper arc? The general rule of thumb is that the ball should go at least 6 to 8 feet above the rim. It is so important for this arc to be high because the target, which is the opening of the rim, is much bigger when the ball is falling more in a downward angle than if it comes straight in. If you will shoot your all your balls in a higher arc, you will see a big improvement in the number of baskets you will make.

Again, once you have this ideal arc or trajectory in your conscious mind, you just let your "other than conscious mind" figure out and learn to actually do it. When you are practicing shooting, pay

33

attention to the trajectory and compare it to your ideal. Then imagine or visualize the perfect arc if your ball didn't go the way you wanted it to.

When you are practicing and you miss a shot, you need to re-program it every time so that your body will get specific instructions on what to do the next time. Then the next time you shoot from the same position, just let your body figure out how to make it go in. This happens so much better when you focus on the hook and let yourself exhale and relax properly as you are shooting, instead of trying hard to make the shot.

In the next part, I am going to tell you a very specific technique that will really improve your shooting. You won't want to miss this one.

Lesson No. 6: An Undervalued Technique: Holding the Follow Through

Have you ever heard of holding your arm and hand on your follow through after you shoot? This is one of the "dirty little secrets" of shooting. Holding after you shoot means that your arm, wrist and hand come to an absolute relaxed stop until your ball actually gets to the basket. What this will do for you is to help take away your physical reaction to your shot. The natural tendency is to react in some way. When you make it truly OK to miss your shot (or make it) without judgment then your body can and will take over for you.

Let me tell you an interesting story. I went to a Bellingham Slam semi-pro basketball game in my home town and I was watching them warm up. There was this one player who actually held his arm and wrist up on his follow through every time until the ball got to the rim. He started shooting baskets close to the side line and behind the three point line. He then proceeded to shoot baskets all the way around the three point line to the other sideline. He must have taken 10 to 12 shots. What was amazing was that he did not miss a shot. All 10 to 12 balls went in. Now maybe you can say that holding his arm until the ball reached the basket was not the reason why he made all of his shots, but just maybe it was a huge factor.

Unfortunately, he did not get any play time in that game. I did want to see if he was able to hold his arm that long when he was actually playing. I also wanted to see how well he shot under the pressure of having his opponent in his face, but there was no doubt that he could really shoot.

After the game I talked to him and he told me of another reason to hold your follow through. Because your arm is still "out there" there is a more likely chance of being fouled. You also need to hold your follow through even on a layup as the chances of being fouled then is much greater. Just the possibility of being fouled more so you can get a free shot would be worth learning this, don't you think?

Lesson No. 7: Shooting on the UpForce

Shooting on the UpForce is one of the critical techniques that I discovered from Tom Nordland's Swish method of shooting. If you are really serious about improving your shooting, getting Tom's Swish DVD is required. Go here to learn more.

Zen-Sational Basketball Shooting

http://www.swish22.com/

Here is what the swish method is all about.

"The Swish approach to shooting is unique and very effective. It's in many ways different from how this skill is normally taught, and that is a good thing. Few players in this country can shoot well any more, and the fault lies partly in how it's coached.

"Swish is both a great technique of shooting (it describes how the great shooters have always done it) and a way to coach it, both to yourself and for others. It breaks down shooting into its simple, basic parts and then shows you how to put it back together."

CHECK OUT THESE VIDEOS!

http://www.swish22.com/assets/ATasteOfSwish_AF.html

And

GO HERE TO ORDER

http://www.swish22.com/store

So let's get back to shooting on the UpForce and what that means.

Shooting on the UpForce means that when you release the ball your body movement is still going up. If you watch many players when they execute a jump shot, you will notice that they release the ball when they are moving down from their jump. By releasing the ball as you are moving up, generates not only more relaxed power, but it allows you to shoot with the arms in a more relaxed and consistent manner.

This is all I'm going to say about shooting on the UpForce here because, like I said, if you are really serious about improving your shooting, getting Tom Nordland's Swish method and DVD is an absolute must.

His technique and how he teaches it is incredibly simple and easy to learn. When you add his technique to the mental approach I give you here, you will see amazing results in your shooting stats.

Lesson No. 8: Focus On the Hook? What's That?

Have you ever heard of focusing on the hook? Do you even know what I mean by the hook? If you will look at your rim, you will see that the net is attached to a series of hooks around the rim. These are the hooks that I am talking about. The hook that you will always focus on is the one at the back of the rim. So, no matter where you are on the court, there will always be the hook at the back of the rim.

I learned about focusing on the hook from a book called *Basketball – It's All About The Shot* by Dave Jones. You can download it for free if you want another view of how to shoot a basket using your mind.

Go here to get it.

http://www.innerbasketball.com/downloads1.php

I highly recommend reading this book.

Now that you know what the hook is, you can now answer the following question correctly. What do you think is the most important thing to focus on when you are shooting? I am hoping you said focusing on the hook. Have you ever done this when you shoot? Have you even thought about doing it? Whether you answered yes or no, this is so important because it gives your body the information it needs to make the shot and helps keep destructive thought away.

Notice I did not say that you need to try to make the shot. You need to let your body figure out how this will happen. You just need to focus on the hook. When you are focusing on the hook, your mind will, of course, translate this into the fact that your ball needs to go just over the front rim.

Just saying to focus on the hook is not really the full concept. What I mean by focusing on the hook is that I mean you **consciously see the hook until your ball reaches the rim.** Only by **consciously seeing the rim** will you know for sure that you are focusing on it properly.

When you are in an actual game, this can be difficult because you have the distraction of your opponent wanting to block or interfere with your shot. I do believe, however, that with practice you can learn to focus properly even if a bomb goes off next to you.

There is one time, however, that you will not want to focus on the hook. When you are shooting a bank shot, you will then focus not on the hook but on the point of the backboard where you want your ball to hit.

There are some people, however, who are able to "see" more peripherally. For these people, it may not be as important for them to consciously focus on the hook when they shoot. But, even these players, will need to consciously focus on the hook when practicing so that their body can learn how to make the shot from any position.

Then, in the game, you let the "other than conscious mind" take over.

Lesson No. 9: Breathing: An Unknown But Powerful Technique

In this lesson you will learn something else that you won't hear anywhere else. It is a very powerful technique but you absolutely have to work on it. Just about all my students say it is the most difficult thing to do when you are shooting, but it can be the most incredible one you will do.

Here is a story about this breathing. Some years ago, a person I know had a son who was going to be playing for Western Washington University Varsity Basketball team. Unfortunately, he had some knee issues and had to red shirt that particular year. Anyway, when I was watching him practice, I noticed that he was holding his breath when he shot.

I told his dad about this and asked the dad to tell his son about breathing when he shoots. His son told his dad that breathing had nothing to do with anything so his dad just accepted that his son was not interested in trying it. Well, a few days later his son told him that when he exhaled when he shot he could hardly miss.

This is an extreme case, but you also may see extreme improvement if you will do what you will learn in this lesson.

Zen-Sational Basketball Shooting

Do you know now what the second most important thing to focus on and maybe even the first most important thing to focus on when shooting? I will bet you that you didn't even have breathing in your list of things that you considered. Am I wrong?

After focusing perfectly on the hook, breathing properly when shooting is the second most important thing to focus on. Exhaling when shooting is so important because when you breathe properly it keeps the upper body more relaxed, thereby allowing your body to shoot better.

If any of you have taken a yoga class, you will know that breathing is a big part of getting the full benefit from it. Basketball is no different except that you will be using the breathing to stay in the here and now, as well as using it to help you learn how to keep your "conscious mind" out of the way. And, like yoga, working with your breathing helps you relax properly.

Proper relaxation of all parts of your body when shooting is also very important but proper breathing is the most important part of this relaxation package. I will discuss more of this other part of the relaxation package later. However, you will need to work on the breathing part as much as on focusing on seeing the hook.

The next time you shoot, begin by just being aware of how you breathe as you are shooting. Check to see if you are holding your breath when you release the ball. Without this ability to consciously pay attention to yourself breathing, it will be difficult to work on changing your breathing pattern in the way I describe below.

Once you have the ability to pay attention to your breathing, you can start working on the quality and rhythm of it. Here is what I consider to be the most effective and natural breathing pattern while shooting.

Zen-Sational Basketball Shooting

Using an exhale, start it before you release the ball. This exhale should be a sigh that is long, slow, and relaxed and should continue until the ball reaches the rim, backboard or net. You don't have to concern yourself with your inhales as I guarantee that you will do it.

Exhaling as you release the ball is a very natural way to breathe, so all you have to do is start your exhale before you release the ball, make it smooth and relaxed, and make it longer than usual. It doesn't get any easier than that.

There are three important points to remember. First, no matter what shot you are taking, the exhale should always be very relaxed and is not a forceful blow or exhale. It should actually be a sigh. Second, you should start the exhale before releasing the ball, and third, you should continue exhaling until the ball reaches the net, rim or backboard.

Staying focused on the hook and breathing at the same time is the ultimate thing to do but it is not easy. It takes a lot of work and a lot of letting go but when you can do both together, you will see huge results and maybe even spectacular results.

It will also be difficult to stay with the breathing when you are driving to the basket and your opponent (or the whole team) is in your face and maybe even fouling you. But if you can stay with your breathing and do a relaxed exhale as you shoot even under those conditions, you just may find yourself making the basket even though you get fouled big time.

Just because it may be hard to do, please don't let that keep you from working on your breathing. The results will make it worth the effort.

Here is an exercise for you to do to help with your breathing.

Practice shooting just focusing on your breathing. When I say to work on your breathing when you are shooting, I also mean that you should work on your breathing when practicing lay-ups, or practicing any of your fancy moves while shooting.

While working on your breathing, feel your face and see if it is tense or if you have an expression change. When you exhale properly, your face will be very relaxed. To help you with relaxing your face, have a friend observe your face when you shoot or when you are doing your fancy moves. Many times, you won't be aware of what your face is doing.

As I have said, doing a relaxed exhale while shooting is the most important part of the relaxation package. In the next lesson, I will talk about the other parts of the relaxation package.

Lesson No. 10: Relaxation: Why It Works & How To Do It

Have you ever felt awkward when you shot?

I believe that just about any time you shoot and it feels awkward or hard, you can pretty much narrow the problem down to a relaxation issue.

What do I mean by relaxation? Being properly relaxed when shooting the ball means only using those muscles that are needed to execute the shot and using the right amount of tension. It is not the relaxed way you feel after or during a massage. This proper amount of relaxation and tension is demonstrated when we watch the professionals play and we say, "They make it look so easy."

The problem is that no one knows exactly which muscles those are or what the proper tension is for each shot. The good news is that your "other than conscious mind" knows, or it will learn if you let it.

When you try hard to do something (especially the first time and when learning any new physical skill), you use so many more muscles than you need to and often with much more tension. And you wonder why it takes so long for that new skill to become easy and second nature.

Much of what you need to do is to discover only which muscles that are needed when you shoot. This is accomplished by isolating and being aware of the level of relaxation in some specific part of your body starting with your arm, wrist and fingers and ending with your legs.

Here is the little secret (or maybe a big secret) as to why relaxing works so well. When you are relaxing and not trying to control your body with your conscious mind, your body falls under the supervision of your "other than conscious mind" and it can then take control of your motion using only the necessary muscles.

Your "other than conscious mind" will also figure out exactly how to make the ball travel in the perfect trajectory, the perfect distance, and in the perfect direction. If the body doesn't know, by keeping your conscious mind out of the way and from trying to control your body, your body will learn that much faster.

So, how do you work on using only the muscles you need, and how do you know if you are doing it properly? There are some signs that you can watch for.

Zen-Sational Basketball Shooting

When you shoot and you feel awkward or the shot feels hard to do, it means you are too tense somewhere in your body. If you have ever paid attention to what your face is doing when you shoot the ball, you may notice that it is not relaxed and you are "making a face". That means you are too tense. You also may be holding your breath and/or trying too hard.

When you feel you are too tense somewhere, you first have to isolate where in the body the tension is located. Here are some of the areas, in order of importance, that seem to be common to most players.

- Breathing - holding the breath as you shoot
- Your arm, and/or your wrist, and/or your fingers
- Your face
- Your legs
- Your left hand (your right hand if you are left-handed)
- Your left ear (OK, maybe I am being a little ridiculous)

Once you have determined what area you think may be tense, all you need to do is pay attention to that area when you are shooting. For example, if you think that your fingers or your wrist is too tight, pay attention to your five fingers and wrist as you shoot the ball. Don't forget to feel your left hand, wrist, and fingers if you are right handed. When you work with this awareness on one part of your body at a time, you will discover the ability to become more relaxed.

At the same time you are working on relaxing by paying attention to some part of your body, it is critical that you refrain from trying to do anything about the tension other than letting it be what it will be. The trying leads to more tension. Give yourself the idea of being relaxed and then just let it go. Let your "other than conscious mind" figure out how to shoot the ball into the basket using only the muscles that are truly needed, and get your conscious mind out of the way.

44

As you begin to be able to let go of all the other muscles you don't need when you are shooting the ball, your shooting technique will become more natural and so much easier. Your shot percentage will improve, and you will be using so much less physical effort. I am sure that at times when you have played you have taken a shot that felt absolutely effortless. When this happens, you will know that you are in the state of perfect relaxation. This is what you are striving for. And, all this "letting go" leads to "playing in the zone."

In the next part, I will discuss free throws and how to improve your percentages. Is that something that would be of interest to you?

Lesson No. 11: Make More Free Throws. Guaranteed!

When I watch basketball games, I marvel at how many free throws are missed. Even by players in the NBA. I can't figure out how these unbelievably talented players miss easy free throws over and over again. And all too often these missed free throws cost the team the game.

The good news is that you don't have to miss these shots. The bad news is that I don't believe that most players have a clue as to how to actually make the ball go into the basket. And, I am talking about the pros also.

How do you shoot free throws? Do you have a routine that works when you are under pressure?

Here is a technique that will absolutely help you make those free throws. As you will see, the technique is pretty easy to talk about, but as in anything, you will need to practice this way of shooting. Don't believe it will work? Try it!

The Full Visualization Technique

The full visualization means that you will start your visualization at the end which means at the hook. Then, in your mind have the ball travel back to your body and then visualize the ball going back to the basket.

Here are the details.

Start by focusing on the hook.

Imagine or visualize the trajectory the ball must travel as it moves back to your hand. Remember that the ideal trajectory is where the ball rises at least 6 to 8 feet higher than the rim.

Imagine or visualize your arm and hand shooting the ball, holding your follow through until the ball reaches the rim.

Now start again by imagining or visualizing from the beginning, feeling yourself shooting with a very relaxed arm and hand, again holding your follow through until the ball reaches the rim. Keep visualizing yourself breathing perfectly with a long exhale, seeing the ball travel to the basket in a perfect trajectory and dropping into the basket.

Take a practice shot without the ball just using your arm and hand if you want. When you do it, make sure that you are exhaling relaxed and seeing in your mind the ball going into the basket.

When you actually shoot, **DO NOT TRY TO MAKE THE BASKET.** Just forget about trying and focus on the hook and allow your arm, hand and breathing to be relaxed.

Things You Need To Stop Doing when Shooting Free Throws

Here are some things I see so many players doing as they get ready to shoot free throws. When they do these things it is no wonder they miss so much. Please stop doing these things as they do not help you make the free throw.

Stop bouncing the ball nervously. If you do bounce the ball a few times, make sure you are very relaxed when you do it and stop early enough so that you have time to do your visualization.

Stop spending time looking down and then shoot 1 second later. Focus on the hook only and keep it there.

Stop thinking about trying to make a basket. Trust that your "other than conscious mind" will control your body and make the shot.

Stop thinking about what the score will be if you make or don't make the basket. Just focus on letting go so that your body can make the shot. The score will take care of itself and thinking about it will lead to trying hard which leads to tension which may lead to missing the free throw.

The Quick Visualization Technique

If you are making all of your free throws, you may not need to do the full visualization. But you may still want to do this quick visualization technique every time you shoot free throws. Here is what you are to do.

As you are focusing on the hook, just see the ball traveling in the perfect trajectory and distance to the basket. Maybe even do a practice motion without the ball.

Again, when you actually shoot, **DO NOT TRY TO MAKE THE BASKET.** Just forget about trying and focus on the hook and allow your arm, hand and breathing to be relaxed. You will still want to keep your arm up on your follow through until your ball reaches the rim, net or backboard.

Lesson No. 12: When Shooting Free Throws In Front Of Crowds (Friendly or Hostile) Bother You

Here I will talk about how to shoot free throws in front of crowds whether they are friendly or hostile.

It's fun to play in front of crowds, don't you think?

But what if you don't like it? What if you let the crowd affect your shooting of free throws? How do you deal with it?

Zen-Sational Basketball Shooting

The bottom line is that if you are bothered by crowds, then you are not focusing very well. Your focus needs to stay on the hook and on your breathing. Sounds easy, doesn't it? But when you are in front of a crowd, everything changes and it can keep you from doing what you normally do.

Some people have a specific issue of wanting to look good in front of a crowd. If that applies to you, here are some ideas. Do you think wanting to play well for the crowd is going to actually help you play well? I don't think so and we have talked about the fact that trying to do anything doesn't work very well. However, I do believe that if the crowd is on your side, their energy will help you but you can't depend on the crowd always being on your side.

When you have the feeling that you want to play well for a crowd, your family, your girlfriend, your boyfriend, your spouse, your team, your country, or anyone else, you must keep in mind what it is that you must do in order to actually shoot well. And, you now know that staying focused is the key. When you let any other thoughts of wanting to shoot well for anyone stay in your mind, it leads to trying which leads to being too tense, which in turn keeps you from focusing and playing as well as you could.

So, here is what you can do. The moment you have these or any destructive thoughts, you need to say to yourself, **"CANCEL, CANCEL"**, and replace the thoughts with more productive statements. And one of these statements, which you will say to yourself a million times, is **"I am staying focused on the hook when I shoot, keeping my arm, wrist and fingers relaxed and holding my follow through until the ball reaches the rim. I am breathing with proper relaxation and letting my body shoot."**

As long as we are on crowds, I might as well talk a little about other distractions when you are shooting free throws.

Zen-Sational Basketball Shooting

The first thing to do is to really focus on your breathing as you are standing on the free throw line waiting to shoot. Almost like meditating on it. This means doing slow, deep inhales and exhales with the emphasis on relaxing when you exhale.

What this does is keep you in the here and now and helps to let go of "other thoughts" or "things" that may be distracting to you like the crowd etc. However, it could be an individual yelling at you, or a player on the other team saying something to make you miss. These and more will come into your universe at some time.

The other part to dealing with any of these distractions is to do what I learned in a yoga class many years ago. At the end of the class, the instructor always had us do the corpse posture. If you have ever taken yoga, you know what this is. You just lie down on your back and completely relax every muscle in your body. It really feels good.

As we were just starting to relax, the instructor would have us listen and pay attention to any noise that we heard. Since the class was near an airport and you could always hear cars go by etc, there was always something making noise. The instructor then said to hear this noise and understand that this noise is just part of life and to make it truly OK for it to be there because you have no control over it. Then the instructor said to just let this noise be in the background and now to focus on letting every muscle go and relax.

It really made a difference just to make these distractions a natural part of life. Likewise, make the crowd and what it is doing a natural part of your world and make it OK. Then, like I said earlier, just let it be there and continue to stay focused on the hook when you shoot, keeping your arm, wrist and fingers relaxed and holding your follow through until the ball reaches the rim.

I hope this helps and, in any case, as you play in front of crowds more often, you will get used to it. However, once you get used to crowds, there will always be something else. This is why it would be a good idea to work on and practice these concepts on letting go of any distractions sooner rather than later.

In the next lesson I will explain what you can do when you miss. That is assuming that you do miss. Oh you do miss shots? Then you will want to read this next section.

Lesson No. 13: When You Miss a Shot

Do you know why you miss a shot? If you are like most players in just about all sports, I am willing to bet that you don't.

Do you think if you really knew why you missed, you would be able to fix it? I believe that if you did know the "real" reason, you would then have a chance to improve. However, I don't think that most people know the "real" reason why and therefore they keep missing over and over and when they do improve, it is very slowly at best and only after practicing for a million more hours. I love to exaggerate, don't I?

In a moment, I am going to tell you some reasons why you miss a shot. See if you have ever thought about these reasons and how to fix them. You can do these "fixes" pretty much on the spot when you are practicing but obviously you can't do them during a game or scrimmage.

Zen-Sational Basketball Shooting

You can and should do this when you are practicing or when doing free throws. When you are in an actual game, you can "fix" your shots only when you are on the bench or during the warm up at half time or in the locker room at half time.

The first thing you need to know is where your shot went off. I would suggest that you use this checklist in this order.

- Did I really focus on the hook until my ball reached the rim, net, or backboard?
- Did I breathe properly or did I hold my breath?
- Did my shot feel relaxed?
- Did my arm and hand come to a complete, relaxed stop on the follow through until the ball reached the rim or backboard?
- Did I try to make the basket?
- If I was playing a real game, did my opponent throw my focus off?
- Was I thinking about the score in any way?
- Did I try or think about anything else that may have interfered with making the shot?

After you determine if any of the above happened while you were shooting, you will then need to re-program your shot by visualizing the way you would have wanted it to go. Once you have done this, just forget it and keep letting your body shoot the ball as it is described in earlier lessons.

When you go to shoot again after visualizing, the most important thing to do is to absolutely forget about trying to make it happen. This is the biggest mistake people make after they have imagined and visualized the correction.

Lesson No. 14: Some Powerful Statements

Those of you who are really focusing on the hook well may have noticed that when you miss, many times it is because you have lost your focus on the hook. I know for me, when I play tennis and see the ball and breathe the way I want to, I feel like I just can't miss the shot. This may be true, but I just can't see and breathe the way I want 100% of the time.

If this seems true for you, does this mean that you have to miss the shot every time you lose focus? It may seem that way to you so I have come up with a way to minimize the effect of this lack of focus.

When you are on the bench or just practicing your shots and you are re-programming (visualizing) your shot and re-programming your mental focus on the hook and your breathing, add this phrase to the end: **"No matter how well I see the hook or don't see the hook, no matter how well I breathe or don't breathe, all my shots are still going into the basket."**

You need to remember all the thousands of times you made your shot before you learned how to focus and what to focus on. And sometimes, you even made some really great shots. This means that your body may just be able to make the basket even if your focus is not so good.

Here is another statement you may want to use. **When you make a great shot, why not congratulate your body, pat yourself on the back and say, "That was a great shot, body, keep those shots coming. I will get out of the way and let you continue making these great shots. Just keep them coming."**

I feel that is much better than yelling at yourself to "come on" or to get angry with yourself. Somehow, I don't think that if your girlfriend, boyfriend, your wife or husband, or a friend yelled at you that way, you would want to respond in a really positive way. I know, I wouldn't.

So, be kind and gentle to your body, work with it, and trust that it will make lots of great shots for you. All you have to do is to use the "core principles," and get your conscious mind out of the way.

Lesson No. 15: Why Choke When You Don't Have To

Any time you are in a close game and you miss more shots than you usually do or you miss easy shots that you usually make, you need to take a look at what happened as the end of the game approached. You need to ask yourself, "Did I miss easy shots or shots I usually make, or did my opponent force me into errors by playing really good defense?"

If you missed your shots because your opponent played better defense then the only conclusion as to why you missed more shots is that he or she just out played you on that day. You may want to figure out how your opponent played better, and then figure out a way to overcome your opponent's defense and work on it.

On the other hand, if you missed easy shots or played worse than you did earlier in the game, then you "choked." If you missed more free throws as the time was running out in a close game, then you can figure that you choked under pressure.

54

Zen-Sational Basketball Shooting

The good news is that you can learn to not choke.

Here are some questions you need to ask yourself to determine if you choked:

- As the end of the game got closer, did I think about winning?

- Did I have any thoughts about losing?

- Did I have thoughts that said, "All I have to do is make this free throw" or "If I make this next shot, we will win"?

- Did I have thoughts that said, "I better not miss this free throw or this next shot" or "If I miss this free throw or shot we will lose the game"?

- Did I try hard to make free throws or did I try hard to make the basket when I shot?

- Did I try hard to "not lose"?

Any thought of winning (or losing) as the end of the game approaches is DEATH. Any thought of winning (or losing) at any time of the game is DEATH. Trying hard to make a shot or trying to do anything, especially at this time of the game, is DEATH.

What happens at this time is that you start to try harder, and therefore you start tensing up. As you miss more, you try even harder, you get more tense, and the cycle continues.

So, what do you do? You do the opposite. You relax more (this means that you are trusting your body to make the shots), and you focus on the hook better when you shoot (without trying hard, of course) while you exhale properly and let your body shoot.

The closer the game, the more you want to trust your "other than conscious mind" to make your shots. This means that you focus well, yet keep your conscious mind out of the way and keep it from controlling your shots. And, of course, this happens when you keep your body relaxed.

At the same time, your opponent is doing what you used to do. They are trying harder because at this time of the game they are thinking that making every shot is very important or playing hard defense is important and therefore will most likely be the ones tensing up, making mistakes and choking. I can't tell you how many times I have seen this happen when games get close at the end.

I also see this happen in the second half when a team has a very comfortable lead and then they try so hard to keep that lead or to start trying harder to not lose that they end up losing the game or just barely winning.

Using these techniques really work. However, they may not work every time but that is not a good reason not to work on changing your thought patterns when the games get close.

Lesson No. 16: Six Things You Absolutely Have To Work On When Practicing Your Shooting

1. Keep your focus on **consciously** seeing the hook at the back of the rim as you shoot.
2. Breathe with a relaxed exhale every time you shoot. This includes on all lay ups. This exhale must always start before you release the ball. When doing lay-ups, start the exhale when you take the last two steps before releasing the ball.
3. Hold your follow throw until your ball either hits the rim or your ball goes through the rim. Do this even on lay ups.
4. Make sure the arc of your shots are 6 to 8 feet above the net. Even on lay ups the arc should be higher than normal but not 6 to 8 feet.
5. Release the ball on the up motion or UpForce.
6. Reprogram all missed shots.

The best way to do all of this is every time you warm up. You start out by doing one at a time then work on combining.

If you're having difficulty with one of the things you can choose to work on it in the entire practice or warm up session. You can also always choose to work on two things for an entire practice session or any combination of the above for an entire practice session.

However, the main issue is that you must work on all of these things at some time during your practice as doing these things automatically when you are in a game is what is going to help you learn the fastest and to shoot your best.

What should you do if you become aware of unproductive or destructive thoughts? I will address this next.

Lesson No. 17: Keeping Unproductive or Destructive Thoughts Away

When unproductive thoughts come into your mind, do you know what to do to recover from them? Maybe the first question should be, "Are you even aware of your unproductive thoughts?" Because, only when you are aware of them can you begin to deal with them.

"I really need to make this free throw." "I am playing terrible." "I am missing easy shots." These are examples of unproductive thoughts.

The "official" definition of an unproductive thought is any thought that not only doesn't help you play better but also thoughts that are destructive and will sabotage your play.

Here is how you can deal with these thoughts and you must deal with them immediately. Please don't wait until the game is over. You may need to wait until you are taking a break on the bench, but if there is time while you are playing, you need to change these thoughts.

Here are some more unproductive and destructive thoughts that you will need to be aware of and deal with. There may be many others and you need to be on the lookout for them.

- As the end of the game got closer, did I think about the score or about winning?

Zen-Sational Basketball Shooting

- During the game, did I have any thoughts about losing?

- Did I have thoughts that said, "All I have to do to win is to make this free throw or make just one more basket" or "If I make this next shot we will win the game"?

- Did I have thoughts that said, "I better not miss this free throw" or "If I miss this free throw, we will lose the game"?

- Did I try hard to win or to make more baskets?

- Did I try hard to "not lose"?

Did I hear any "yes" answers? Did you answer yes to all of them? If you answered yes to all of them, you are in serious trouble and we will need to do a frontal lobotomy. Please make an appointment. ☺

Here is the ultimate answer to dealing with these thoughts. It is one that must be taken very seriously if you want to reduce or eliminate playing badly at critical times in the game. So, here it is.

Any thought of winning or losing when the game is close is DEATH. Any thought of winning or losing at any time of the game is DEATH. Trying hard to do anything, especially at this time of the game, is DEATH.

Again, what happens at this time is that you start to try harder, and therefore you start tensing up. As you make more mistakes, you try even harder, you get more tense, and the cycle continues.

So, what do you do? You do the opposite.

The moment you are aware that you had an unproductive thought you say to yourself **"Cancel Cancel"**, or yell internally to yourself as loud as you can **"Stop!"** and then take a sighing exhale. Then make a
59

statement that is productive. The kinds of statements that I am talking about are as follows: **"OK, body, I can't make this shot or free throw. You will have to do it. I will stay out of your way and I will just focus on the hook and breathe properly when I shoot."** Or, **"I am staying focused on the hook when I shoot, keeping my arm, wrist and fingers relaxed and holding my follow through until the ball reaches the rim. I am breathing with proper relaxation and letting my body shoot."**

Please don't use a negative like "I am not going to try to make this next basket or free throw" as they say in NLP circles your subconscious mind does not hear the "not." It just hears "I am going to try ..." and hopefully you know trying doesn't work very well.

The closer the game, the more you want to trust your "other than conscious mind" to make your shots and to play. This means that you focus well, keep your conscious mind out of the way and keep it from controlling your play. And, of course, this happens when your body is relaxed.

So, when you are sitting on the bench or waiting for a free throw to be taken, all you need to do is to remember to re-program any thoughts that do not help you shoot and play your very best.

Lesson No. 18: Do You Shoot Differently in Your Warm-up Than You Do When the Game Starts?

First of all, you must understand what is so different. If you think about it, there are four differences when the game starts. One difference is that now you will have someone in your face when you shoot. Secondly, you won't have all day to set up to shoot as you do when you warm up. Thirdly, there may a lot of time between shots so maybe you could say that you are cold. And the fourthly is that all of a sudden everything is more important. At least, your mind thinks so.

When you are just warming up, it doesn't matter to you if you miss the shot, and you may not be trying hard to aim your shots or even trying hard to make the basket (I hope). You are just shooting the ball.

Once the game starts, you must trick your "conscious mind" into thinking that the game is not any more important than the warm up. Stop trying to aim or make the basket. You (your body) already know how to do this. You did it in the warm up.

Stop trying to use perfect technique. This is not the time for working on your technique.

Stop trying to win or thinking about winning. If your team plays better than your opponent, winning will take care of itself. And, most importantly, read and use the "Mental Game Core Principles." They work.

If you can do these things, the only difference between the warm up and when you start the game will be how good your opponents are on defense and the effect that has on your shots. Of course, you have little control over your opponent.

You should know by now that letting go is always the direction you want to go in when you find yourself not playing well or, in this case, not playing as well as you did in the warm up. As mentioned in the previous paragraph, if all you did was the "Core Principles" you would be in the zone.

Lesson No. 19: How To Decide When To Shoot

Think about when you are warming up. You just **know** when you want to shoot, and without thinking very hard, if at all, you just do it. You **know** this before you even get on the court.

The same applies when you are in a game situation. It is simply a **"knowing"** of when you want to shoot and just doing it. Trying hard, thinking hard, making it important, or trying to force a shot won't work in the long run or when you are under pressure.

Like when you warm up or you are doing drills, you already know in advance where and when you are going to shoot. However, when it comes time to choose where to shoot in a real game, the process is a little different.

The analogy I like to use is this: you need to get to an important appointment and you were a little late getting out of the house and

62

when you went to get the keys to your car, you couldn't find them. So, you panic a little and try as you might, you can't think of where your keys are. But, instead of finding them, you go get your spare set of keys, get into your car and drive away. As you are driving and now knowing that you will be able to get to your appointment in plenty of time, you relax.

Then out of nowhere, you remember that your keys to your car were in the top drawer of your desk. You were not trying to remember and the thought just came to you.

Well, the same approach needs to be used when deciding when to shoot. **Let the thought come to you and then you just see the hook and exhale properly as you let your body shoot. This also means that this thought is your first thought.**

Thinking hard about when you think you should shoot is death and may cause you to miss even an easy shot, as it tenses up your body and tends to keep your focus away from the hook and your breathing. When you are thinking too much, missing shots may happen way too many times especially if you are playing in an important game or if the game is almost over and the score is really close.

There will be times when you will decide to shoot at a time that was inappropriate. What do you do about it and how can you learn to make better choices? If you are just scrimmaging you can't stop and reprogram your shot. If you are playing in a game, the obvious time to "fix" this is when you are sitting on the bench. Just calm your mind and think about the inappropriate shot and see yourself making a better decision. Then just let it go. Your "other than conscious mind" will take over as you let these decisions come to you and you will learn to make better and better decisions on when to shoot.

Another way to help you program yourself when to shoot is to watch the best shooter on your team and/or the best shooter on the other team and watch when they decide to shoot. If you think they chose a good time to shoot, then imagine yourself in the same situation and you are deciding to shoot in those same situations.

Still, it does take practice figuring out what I mean by **knowing** and how to let this **knowing** come to you. Unfortunately, I can't really tell you how to do this except to tell you to keep your mind calm and clear so that these thoughts can, in fact, get through.

I can tell you that when you do learn to do it, you will be able to shoot from anywhere you want effortlessly and without thinking, which is to say by instinct. And, the more you work with all of these concepts I have given you, the more it will become easier for you to understand what **knowing** means.

Lesson No. 20: Don't waste Time When You Are Sitting On the Bench Waiting To Go Into The Game Again

What do you do when you are sitting on the bench waiting to play? Do you just watch your team mates play or do you work on your game mentally? Maybe you won't need to or want to work on your game mentally a great deal while you are sitting down, but if it would help you play better thereby helping your team to win, wouldn't you want to explore what you could do?

When you are sitting on the bench, you can use this time to calm and clear your mind, do a relaxing breath which would be a deep, long sighing exhale and imagine and visualize any changes you would like to make in your play.

This can be a very powerful time for you if it is done properly. And remember, once you get back into the game, keep letting your body play with perfect focus, breathing and relaxation.

Lesson No. 21: A Short Review of What To Do When You Play In Your Games

When you play games here is a summary of what needs to be done to fully play the mental game and play up to your potential.

Make the "Core Principles" the most important thing that you do.

Make sure you don't think about your technique. If you feel you need some help with a particular shot, visualize and re-program it mentally when you are on the bench or, if you are just practicing, take a practice shot without the ball, and then forget about it and go back to doing the "Core Principles".

Every time you miss a shot and you have a few seconds, re-program and visualize the ball going into the basket, then forget about it and go back to doing the "Core Principles".

Remove all judgments (or at least keep them to a minimum). When you judge, it leads to trying which leads to tension, which leads to missing shots.

If you miss a shot, let it go and encourage your body to learn to make it the next time through visualizing and re- programming.

If you make a good shot, give your body credit, don't try to do it again but tell your body to keep those good shots coming.

If you think about winning at any time but especially at the end of a game, take a deep breath, sigh your exhale and say **"Cancel Cancel"** letting those thoughts go. Go back to doing the "Core Principles".

Lesson No. 22: Have You Done Your Foundation Work?

Have you purchased any of the programs that I have recommended to help your play? Or, at least taken a look at them?

I don't recommend these programs lightly. They absolutely will help you play better basketball.

Here is a list of these programs. Please consider getting them. They will be well worth the cost.

http://basketball.intelligym.com - The Basketball IntelliGym™ is the first training program in the world that dramatically improves basketball game-intelligence skills. Whether you are trying to make your junior or high school basketball team, improve your play on the playground or get a college scholarship, the IntelliGym™ will help

66

you get there. Go to their web site and watch the short video about what this program can do for you.

Tom Nordland's Swish method of shooting.

http://www.swish22.com/

If you are really serious about improving your shooting, getting Tom's Swish DVD is required.

As you may recall, I talked about Tom's Swish method in Lesson No. 7 but I wanted to give you another chance to take a look at it just in case you didn't look at it or purchase it before.

Here is what the swish method is all about.

"The Swish approach to shooting is unique and very effective. It's in many ways different from how this skill is normally taught, and that is a good thing. Few players in this country can shoot well any more, and the fault lies partly in how it's coached.

"Swish is both a great technique of shooting (it describes how the great shooters have always done it) and a way to coach it, both to yourself and for others. It breaks down shooting into its simple, basic parts and then shows you how to put it back together."

CHECK OUT THESE VIDEOS!

http://www.swish22.com/assets/ATasteOfSwish_AF.html

And

GO HERE TO ORDER

http://www.swish22.com/store

ANOTHER TERRIFIC HOW TO SHOOT VIDEO BY RICK PENNY

Discover The Proven Technique That Provides The Quickest & Smoothest Release Possible!

"Rick Penny is the purest shooter I have seen at any level. He has developed a shooting video that can benefit anyone who seriously wants to learn how to shoot, quickly and efficiently. His explanations are simple and understandable. I certainly recommend this video ... It is very effective and reasonably priced."

Coach Jerry Stone
Won National Championship at Midland College
(Coached NBA players Spud Webb and Mookie Blaylock)

Is There A Better Way To Shoot?
YES! What trend do you see in NBA & College games today? Declining shooting percentages, right? We know athletes are now bigger and stronger than in the past, so why are percentages going down? There is something fundamentally wrong with the shooting techniques we see in the game today!

BUY RICK'S PROGRAM HERE

http://www.onemotionbasketball.com

I have another question for you. Have you read this book all the way through? Have you read it more than once since you bought it?

Someone told me that a very small percentage of people who actually buy books ever read them. Now, I know that is not true for you and that you have read this book 100's of times by now, right?

So, please do your homework. Read my book all the way through again and get the programs I have told you about in this lesson. I will be giving you a surprise test next week and if you don't pass, you will have to go shoot 10,000 half court shots until they all go in.

Lesson No. 23: How Well Are You Doing the Core Principles?

Are you reading the Core Principles before every game and even before your practices?

This is an absolute must as in just this one section you will find all you need to do to play out of your mind. Everything else I talk about (except for the Lessons on non- mental stuff) is centered around these Core Principles.

So, please keep my book in your bag so you can read them often and really begin to use them. They are very powerful.

If you can do these principles completely, you will have the mental game mastered. However, if you have been working with these principles for any period of time, you will see that like any worthwhile skill, it takes practice and letting go.

Please use this lesson as a reminder for you to read the Core Principles often and read them at the very least before every important game, and continue to make them the "only" things you do when you play.

If you are not making these principles the most important thing you do when you play, you are missing "the key" to playing the mental game.

Lesson No. 24: Why Losing or Missing Shots Is Good

When I'm working with a new student, their reaction to missing shots is often comments like "I played terrible" or "I should have made those free throws." Have you ever heard yourself say either of these two statements or something similar?

My first response to "I played terrible" is to ask, "What did you do when you were on the court or when you were sitting on the bench to turn your play around?" Did you re-program or visualize your shots going in? In my opinion, this is the difference between playing the mental game the way I see it and playing basketball the traditional way. 95% (or more) of the players do not have a clue as to why they miss shots or how to fix their shots on the spot. No wonder these players get angry or frustrated. But you know better now. You just need to remember to do it.

So, let's say that you did play terrible. You need to ask yourself, "What part of my shot was not working?" Usually, it was only one shot like the free throws that was off that day or you made one "bad" play and you translated that into "everything was terrible." Once you have isolated where or which shot went wrong, I then ask, "Were you aware of this while you were playing?" and then, "What should you have done about it?" And finally, I will ask, "What can you do about it now that the game is over?"

70

Zen-Sational Basketball Shooting

I am hoping that you can see what I am doing with my questions. I am helping to isolate the problem so that you can do something about it the next time you are playing as well as go out and practice the shot or shots that were weak or not working very well. But, to just say that "I played terrible" is not helpful.

Sometimes my students will say, "We should have won," I ask them why. They may say that, "We were ahead and lost (choked)," or "We are a better team" or "they got lucky", or "they were not very good at defense," or "We just didn't play well" or any number of things about the game. I tell them, "No, you should not have won because, for whatever reason, your opponent played better than you did and you need to figure out how you contributed to this loss."

If you have ever said these things, once you figure out what your part in the loss was, you can then go and practice the shots you were missing or work on your defense etc. Also, once you understand your opponent was actually better than you were, I would tell you, "If you don't like the fact that your opponent was better than your team, then you need to shoot 50 million more shots so that you improve." Of course, I believe that while you are shooting these 50 million shots, you will improve that much faster if you focus on the "Core Principles" of the mental game and practice the other things in this book.

The whole point of losing or shooting badly is that you get to find out where your weaknesses are. If you played a two year old, you could just about do anything and you would win. When you lose, it should be an incentive for you to go out and shoot those 50 million more shots so that the next time you will shoot better.

When you play a very weak team it does not help you improve (well maybe a little bit) but when you play a better team, it helps you find out where your weakness are so that you can improve and fix them.

71

And, just for the record, as soon as you think that you have fixed your weakness, another one is presented to you the next time you lose.

So really take the time to find out why you didn't shoot or play well and then go and practice using the metal game principles. You will find that your game will continue to improve and maybe you won't have to actually shoot 50 million more shots.

Lesson No. 25: Cause and Results: What is this all about?

So many times when I am teaching, I will ask my student what happened when they missed a particular shot. And, many times they will say, they did this or didn't do that, were too tense or any other of the many physical things that can go wrong when you miss a shot.

Do you know how I answer them? I tell them that these are all things that, in fact, happened, but that they are the result and not the cause of missing. Yes, maybe they were too tense, and yes the tension made you miss the shot, but there is something that caused the tension in the first place. Let's take a look at how this all works.

It is really important that you find what is really causing you to miss because if you don't, how are you going to change or fix it. Fixing the result won't work for very long. It just keeps coming back.

The analogy I like to use is this. If you are walking down a dark alley late at night in a bad section of town, you would, most likely, get pretty tense and start really looking around or calling 911 if you heard a noise. And, no matter what you did, you would have a really hard time relaxing until you were safe at home. So, yes, you were tense, but it was the result of something, not the cause. The cause was the fact that you were in a dangerous place and heard a noise.

Well, unless you find out what is causing you to be tense when you miss a shot, re-programming yourself to relax or telling yourself to do this or that, won't work until the cause is eliminated. Yes, re-programming yourself to relax may work in the short run, but the tension will come back over and over again until you deal with the real cause.

Do you know what some of the obvious causes are that will result in just about every kind of error? How about "trying" to make the ball go into the basket? How about "trying" to win or to not lose? How about "trying" to make a free throw or just "trying" to make a shot the next time you get a chance to shoot? Maybe even "trying" to shoot correctly. How about thinking about letting your team down if you don't play perfectly or if you make a mistake late in the game?

Are you nodding your head as you read these possible causes? I think you get the idea here. Now you have a huge advantage over the other players out there. You now know how to really "fix" what you did wrong. Just let go and let your body play and shoot.

Just re-program or visualize, or talk to yourself about releasing these unproductive ideas or thoughts and get back into focusing and executing the Core Principles.

When you fix your missed shots by really dealing with the cause, you will find that you will not be making these same errors over and over again.

Lesson No. 26: The Value of Playing "Big Games" or Tournaments

Do you like playing in the "big games" or in tournaments? If you don't, you may want to re-think this. Tournaments and "big games" will help you immensely with learning and improving your mental game. It is like taking on-going "final exams" and by looking at the results of these tests, you will learn so much about how your mind and body work together.

"Big Games" and tournaments bring out how powerful your mind is and how much it wants to control your play. Only through important games and tournaments will you have the opportunity to put your mind in its right place.

Notice I haven't said anything about winning. Important games bring to the table the thought that all of a sudden winning is important. Of course, by now we know that thinking about winning when we are playing is **"DEATH"** to playing well and important games are the best environment in which to work on letting go of winning. Remember what I said about John Wooden never talking to his players about winning? He only talked to his players about doing their best and only doing what they needed to do to play their very best.

"Big Games" and tournaments are important because, for some unknown factor, you will improve your game just by osmosis. How this happens I don't know. Just being around other teams and watching the other players somehow improves your own game. Be sure that you guard against trying too hard to play well.

In tournaments (unless you win the finals), you get to play against a better team than yours as well as a wide range of players. When you lose (and sometimes even when you win) you can look at it as a terrific learning opportunity. And for you personally, you will discover where your weaknesses are so you can work on them.

In tournaments or "big games", you get to see how you stack up against other players who may be better than you and who bring to the table a form of defense that keeps you from shooting well. This can be important as this will expand your experience and "force" you to play better.

To sum up, make important games and tournaments something to look forward to so you can "test" how well you play under pressure and as a way of really improving not only your mental game, but your physical game as well.

Lesson No. 27: Use These Defensive Moves

I'm going to move away from shooting in this lesson and talk a little bit about defense.

I go to most of the men's and women's basketball games at Western Washington University. In one of the women's games, there was a woman player on the opponents team who really stood out as a defensive player. I started to watch her play to figure out why she was so good on defense. After watching what she was apparently doing, I then started watching one of the men on the Western

Washington team who was also an outstanding defensive player to see if there were any similarities.

Here is what I found.

First of all, when they were guarding a player who had the ball, every time that person passed the ball their arm moved in the direction of the pass. Even though most of the time their arm moved after the ball was passed, there were times that they were able to move their hands early enough to block or deflect the pass.

While they were waiting for the ball to be passed, they were also attempting to knock the ball out of the hands of the person they were guarding. Of course, you have to be a little cautious so you don't foul too many times but that doesn't mean that you stop trying to hit the ball out of your opponent's hand.

Knowing what I know about reaction time, when you do this you need to keep your arms and hands very loose because only when your arms are loose will your reaction time be at its fastest. Keeping your arms and hands loose when your legs have to move very quickly when you are guarding a player is difficult but you must learn to isolate your upper body so it can move quickly and stay relaxed while you're legs are moving fast.

The other thing I noticed was that these outstanding defensive players seem to have eyes in the back of their head as they knew where the ball was at all times. This means that many times when the ball was passed to the person they were guarding, they began to move toward the ball the moment it was passed and as a result sometimes they will were able to pick the ball off. I also saw them moving towards the ball even when the ball wasn't being passed to the person they were guarding.

How they kept track of the ball and the person they were guarding at the same time, I don't know. However, maybe just having and keeping the thought that you need to do both will, in fact, help you develop eyes in the back of your head.

So when you are on defense, work on keeping your hands and arms very relaxed and be moving your hands every time in the direction that the ball is being passed and work on keeping track of where the ball is at all times and I will guarantee you that your defensive abilities will improve. And, of course, as a result you may find yourself stealing that many more balls.

Do you know for sure if you are playing the mental game properly? In the next part, I will give you all of "the signs" so that you will know without a doubt.

Lesson No. 28: How to Know If You Are Playing The Mental Game Properly

Do you think you are playing the mental game properly? How do you know?

I have heard from players who have said that are playing the mental game. However, if you watch them play, they really aren't playing the inner game at all. There must be some way to know if you are on the right track.

I assume that by now you have read all of the lessons on the mental parts in this book and hopefully you have begun to put these lessons into practice. You may also be "sick to death" of hearing about focusing on the hook, breathing, letting go, relaxing, and the Core Principles. I hope not.

I go over and over these so many times because we have learned all of our lives to try hard, make it happen, beat your opponent, etc and it will take some serious effort to "correct" these thought patterns. With repetition, I am re-enforcing these new patterns of thought and focus.

You can see that there are not that many things you need to do to play the mental game. Using the Core Principles when you play is really all there is to it. You just need to strip away all the unproductive thoughts that get in your way but it is always nice to know if you are playing the mental game properly, or at least making progress.

Here are some questions you can ask yourself which will give you the knowledge that you are on the right track.

- Does your play improve during the game?

- Have you focused on the hook until the ball reaches the rim for at least one shot during the game?

- Has your follow through stayed up until the ball reached the rim for at least one ball?

- Have you felt yourself exhaling properly for at least one shot during the game?

- Have you re-programmed any of your misses either in practice or in the game?

- Have you been aware of any unproductive thoughts and had the presence of mind to stop, say cancel, cancel, and re-program?

- Even if you are not able to focus very well, are you constantly re-programming yourself to see the hook on every shot and working with letting go more and more?

- Are you making the mental game the most important thing to do when you play? I am talking about using the Core Principles.

Any 'yes' answer to the above questions should tell you that you are on the path of playing the mental game. As I have said before, this is a lifelong process. Assuming that you are continuously working on it and are making it important, the improvement in focusing and letting go will continue until you retire from the game. When you work with this aspect of basketball, you will also find that your enjoyment of the game will be greatly enhanced.

Lesson No. 29: How to Know If You Are Actually Improving?

In the last lesson, you learned how to know if you are playing the mental game properly. In this lesson, you're going to learn if you are improving as an overall player. Yes, you can use just the normal stats that are figured for you, but there are better ways which I am going to give to you here.

Have you ever heard of taking the normal stats and putting them into a formula which will then show you where you stand not only compared to yourself but compared to others? And when you look at these stats over a period of time, you will be able to see how much you have improved.

There are two points systems that I am going to tell you about.

Danny Miles' Point System

The first point system was developed by a coach named Danny Miles. He has coached for 38 years at Oregon Tech university where he accumulated 876 career wins which is 6th all time on all collegiate levels. His team was a two Time National champion and two times he was a national coach of the year.

Without going into a huge amount of detail about how his point system is figured, you can go to www.breakthroughbasketball.com and get Danny Miles *Value Point System And A Daily Drills* booklet. However , here I will give you the main formula for figuring the points and at the end of this lesson I will give you an easy way to calculate these points. Here is the formula:

```
Points+Rebounds+2x(Assists)+2x(Steals+Blocks)
-------------------------------------------------
2x(FG Missed)+FT Missed+2x(Fouls)+ 2x(Turnovers)

FG = Field Goals
FT = Free Throws
```

```
SCALE

     COLLEGE (MENS)                WOMENS & HIGH SCHOOL

     EXCELLENT: 1.75+              1.50+
     VERY GOOD: 1.50-1.74          1.25-1.49
          GOOD: 1.25-1.49          1.00-1.24
          FAIR: 1.00-1.24          0.75-0.99
    NEEDS WORK: UNDER 1.00         UNDER 0.75
```

Chuck Randall's Point System

The next point system was developed by a coach at Western Washington university named Chuck Randall.

Chuck was voted the Coach of the Century at Western Washington University. That pretty much says it all about what kind of basketball coach he was and about his record.

Chuck developed this point value system to help him determine not only who his starting 5 would be, but in recruiting players to his team. Although he did not follow his point value system 100% of the time, these stats were very important in helping win games.

To learn a little more about Coach Randall, take a look at this video on YouTube.

http://www.youtube.com/watch?v=uBHyC74mB_Y

And go to the web site,

www.myimpossibledreamchuckrandall.com

Without going into a long technical description as to how all Chuck's points are figured, I will give you the general ideas.

81

Zen-Sational Basketball Shooting

A player gets one point for the number of points scored with bonus points given if their shooting percentage is higher than 50% and have points taken away if the percentage is lower. The same is true for free throws except that the shooting percentage must be 75% or higher to get bonus points. Then you get 2X the number of Offensive rebounds, 1 point for every Defensive Rebound, 2X for Assists, 2X for blocks, and 2X for steals. You get points deducted for Personal Fouls, 2X for every Turn Over.

If the player has less than 10 minutes of play time, the stats per minute is meaningless and it will not be figured.

One thing that is different with Chuck's point system is that you get two stats. One is the total stats and one is the stats per minute of play assuming, of course, that the player plays more than 10 minutes. By figuring the per minute stat, it gives you an indication of how you're doing even if you don't play as much as another player.

Remember I said earlier that I would give you an easy way to figure these stats. I have a program on my computer that computes the stats for you. I just have to enter the normal stats once and the computer compiles both Danny's and Chuck's points. I can't put a sample print out in this book because of the formatting of the printout, but if you would like to take a look at a sample, please go to this web page.

http://www.innerbasketball.com/download_point_system.php

If you would like to have these stats figured for you, send me the normal stats that are compiled for you and I will send to you the first printout of the points for free. Send to david@innerbasketball.com

If you are a coach and would like to have the stats for your team after each game, I would only charge you $7.00 per game and you would get them e-mailed to you within 24 hours in most cases.

Lesson No. 30: What Is EFT ?

Ever heard of EFT?

The other information that you get with this book is the Emotional Freedom Technique (EFT) that I customized for basketball. Have you downloaded the EFT Scripts and used them?

If you have not yet downloaded them, you will need to go here to download the scripts.

www.innerbasketball.com/downloads1.php

I knew about EFT for a long time but it was being used for non-sports issues. Then I found a person who was using it for sports with a section on using it for tennis. I purchased the e-book for $40 to see what it was all about and found it lacking so I wrote my own

"scripts" just for tennis, basketball and baseball. The basketball scripts you get free with this book.

I Paid $197 So You Wouldn't Have To.

I also ran across another person who had some EFT techniques for tennis (and other sports) and it cost $197. I went ahead and purchased it because I figured if they were charging this much it must be really good.

Zen-Sational Basketball Shooting

It turned out this e-book encompasses a lot more than just the EFT techniques for a particular sport. I also felt the scripts on tennis were still missing some important parts but in general this book was pretty good. They just were not as good as my scripts. At least according to my way of thinking.

Please don't think these scripts are not valuable just because you get them for free.

The 8 EFT scripts can be used very effectively with a little study and you get them free without spending the $197 or even $40.

You can also use the basic EFT for just about anything.

I want to help you play your very best and by giving you these extra tools, it will speed up your improvement. I also believe that by learning about EFT it can help you in other areas of your life.

If you want to explore EFT (or Tapping) and how to use it in other areas of your life, please go to this website for The Tapping Solution.

www.thetappingsolution.com

Here you can get DVDs etc and learn how to use this incredible tool in any area of your life. It is a very powerful tool as you will see when you look into it.

Below are a couple more places to go to get information on this tapping technique.

www.bradyates.net - go here for Brad Yate's website.

Go to **www.emofree.com** to learn more about tapping.

There is a bigtime private baseball coach that uses this technique as the centerpiece of his coaching and I have personally seen a video of
84

a big league professional baseball player using this technique. He was caught on a TV camera and the announcers did not have a clue what he was doing, but I doubt that he would be doing it if he thought it wasn't helpful.

Now that you know a little bit about EFT, please download them and start using my scripts for your basketball game.

Lesson No. 31: Prepare Yourself Before You Play and Analyze Your Shooting After You Play

Before The Match

1. Did you read the Core Principles 10-15 minutes before the game? _____
2. Did you do any mind calming or meditation before the game? _____
3. Did you pre-program any strategies before the game? _____
4. Did you warm up before the game using proper breathing and focusing on the hook? _____
5. Did you warm up before the game using proper technique of holding your follow through, proper arc, and proper releasing on the UpForce?

_____

On Seeing the Hook During the Game

1. Did you consciously see the hook until your ball reached the rim on at least one of your shots?

   _____

2. If you saw at the hook on at least one shot, did you make seeing the hook on every shot a priority?

   _____

3. What % of the time were you able to see the hook the way you know it should be seen?

   _____

4. After you missed a shot and were sitting on the bench, did you reprogram seeing the hook?

   _____

5. When you miss a shot, you need to find out if there were any patterns as to why you missed. Do you think that maybe you were missing shots because you didn't see the hook properly? _____

6. On a scale of 1 to 10, how important is **consciously** seeing the hook to you?

   _____

7. If seeing the hook is important to you, what is keeping you from making it more important and focusing on doing it more?

   _____

8. If you just forgot to work on seeing the hook when you shot and especially when you missed a shot, what strategies can you use to help you remember the next time you play in a game?

   _____

9. If you really desired to see the hook well and it was your intention to see the hook well but just couldn't do it during a game, what is going on with you mentally that keeps you from doing it the way you want?

_____

On Breathing During the Game

1. Were you able to exhale before you shot the ball and then allow it to continue until the ball reached the rim at least once? _____

2. If you were able to breathe on more than one shot, what % of the time were you able to exhale properly. _____

3. When you miss a shot, you need to find out if there were any patterns as to why you missed. Do you think that maybe you were missing shots because you didn't breathe properly or that you held your breath? _____

4. On a scale of 1 to 10, how important is breathing when you shoot to you? _____

5. If breathing is important to you, what is keeping you from making it more important and focusing on doing it more?

_____

6. If you just forgot to work on your breathing when you played and especially when you missed a shot, what strategies can you use to help you remember

the next time you play in a game?

_____

7. If you really desired to breathe properly and it was
your intention to breathe properly but just couldn't
do it during a game, what is going on with you
mentally that keeps you from doing it the way you
want?

_____

On Relaxing And Holding Your Wrist And Fingers While Shooting in a Game

1. Do you think that you were able to hold your arm, your
wrist and fingers until the ball reached the rim on at
least one shot?

_____

2. Do you think that you were able to relax your arm, your
wrist and fingers as you held your follow through on at
least one shot?

_____

3. When warming up before a game and at half time warm
up, did you ever take a practice shot without the ball
just keeping your grip and wrist extremely
relaxed?_____

4. If you found that your grip and wrist was very tight and
you were having difficulty relaxing it, did you not only
take practice shots without the ball, feeling the wrist

and fingers but did you make it really important?_____

5. Do you think that you ever held your finish until the ball reached the rim on at least one ball when shooting? And, how about holding the finish even on lay ups?_____

On Shooting with the Proper Arc

1. Were you able to shoot with the proper arc (6 to 8 feet above the rim) at least once? _____

2. If you were able to shoot with the proper arc on more than one shot, what % of the time were you able to have the proper arc? _____

3. When you miss a shot, you need to find out if there were any patterns as to why you missed. Do you think that maybe you were missing shots because you didn't have the proper arc? _____

4. On a scale of 1 to 10, how important is having a proper arc when you shoot to you? _____

5. If having a proper arc is important to you, what is keeping you from making it more important and focusing on doing it more?

   _____

6. If you just forgot to be aware of your arc when you played and especially when you missed a shot, what strategies can you use to help you remember the next time you play in a game?

   _____

7. If you really desired to have a proper ark and it was your intention to have a proper arc but just couldn't do it during a game, what is going on with you mentally that keeps you from doing it the way you want?

_____

On Shooting On The UpForce

1. Were you able to shoot on the UpForce at least once? _____

2. If you were able to shoot on the UpForce on more than one shot, what % of the time were you able to shoot on the UpForce? _____

3. When you miss a shot, you need to find out if there were any patterns as to why you missed. Do you think that maybe you were missing shots because you didn't shoot on the UpForce? _____

4. On a scale of 1 to 10, how important is shooting on the UpForce when you shoot? _____

5. If shooting on the UpForce is important to you, what is keeping you from making it more important and focusing on doing it more?

_____

6. If you just forgot to be aware of shooting on the UpForce when you played and especially when you missed a shot, what strategies can you use to help you remember the next time you play in a game?

_____

7. If you really desired to shoot on the UpForce and it was your intention to do so but just couldn't do it during a game, what is going on with you mentally that keeps you from doing it the way you want?

_____

On Reprogramming Your Shots (When sitting on the bench)

1. Did you take at least one practice shot without the ball after you missed a shot in the warm up? _____

2. If you did take a practice shot without the ball, did you reprogram seeing the ball go where you wanted it to as well as take a very relaxed shot? _____

3. On a scale of 1 to 10, how important to you is reprogramming your shots when you miss? _____

4. If reprogramming your shots works and is important to you, what is keeping you from making it more important and focusing on doing it more?

_____

5. If you just forgot to reprogram your shots when you missed, what strategies can you use to help you remember to reprogram and visualize the next time you play a match?

_____

Other Things To Consider

1. If you ever found yourself thinking about winning or losing or any other unproductive thoughts, did you use the "Cancel, Cancel" or the "STOP" technique to stop these thoughts in their tracks? _____

2. When you're sitting on the bench, did you ever take a very relaxing exhale to calm and clear your mind and body and then re-focused on doing the Core Principles?

_____

3. Did you let your opponent's attitude or behavior get to you? _____ (Remember, you are only playing the ball and your opponent, not their personality)

4. Did you let any other distractions get to you? _____

Lesson No. 32: What To Do When You Have A Question And Don't Know The Answer (The Wondering Technique)

Have you ever lost something and then after you gave up looking for it, the answer just came to you as to where it was. What about when you forgot someone's name and later in the day when you were doing something else, the name came into your mind? This same power of the mind is what we tap into when we use the "Wondering Technique."

Zen-Sational Basketball Shooting

This is one of the terrific concepts I learned from Dave Dobson who was an absolute master of Neural Linguistic Programming commonly known as NLP. Here is one of many many ways you can use this technique.

If you are not shooting very well and you can't figure out what you need to change, you would say to your "other than conscious mind", "I wonder what I can change so that I will be more effective." Or you could say, "I wonder what I could do to shoot better." Then you just relax and let the answer come to you.

Here is the reasoning behind this technique. Back in the old days when we were on the phone and someone tried to call us, they got a busy signal because we didn't have "call waiting" then. There was no way that the person calling you could get through and you didn't even know that someone was trying to call you.

Trying hard to think about what to do differently is like being on the phone, and when the answer does come, your answer will get a busy signal and not get through because your mind is too active. So just relax your Conscious Mind and let the answer come to you.

With practice, this can be a very powerful tool. And you don't have to limit it to basketball. You can use this technique for any issue in your life that you need answers for.

Lesson No. 33: Does Being Complimented Or Being Congratulated Really Help You To Play Better?

Giving compliments to or congratulating a teammate or receiving compliments or congratulating from the coach or teammate during a game seems like a good idea, doesn't it? After all, you have to do something to get yourself to either pick up the pace and/or play better, don't you? And, you see everyone doing it, don't you? This is especially true in the final minutes and all you have to do is to make a free throw.

I am here to tell you why this may not work so well unless you translate it into a more productive thought. And, if all this congratulating worked, you would see the person who was congratulated the most be the best player on the team.

So, what happens when you get compliments or are congratulated for your shot etc. They are saying to your conscious mind, "Great shot, Make it happen again." The problem is that if you let your conscious

mind take the credit, it will then keep on trying harder to play and shoot better.

Your conscious mind will take back control of your play. It wants to take credit for making the great play. It then tries to shoot the ball as well or better again the next time and it just may lead to you missing more shots or making more mistakes. The body tenses up and misses

94

shots for no apparent reason because the conscious mind does not know how to make the body shoot well. It just thinks it does, but really only the "other than conscious mind" does.

Here is the sad part. Sometimes these congratulation comments works. Sometimes all this trying works at the beginning of the game or at other times when making the shot isn't so important. However, when the game gets tight, if you really analyze it, you just may see that at those times it just doesn't work and, in fact, you may play worse.

And what is even sadder, is that sometimes getting a compliment even works when the game is close and then the conscious mind then tells you, "See, you need to have me control your body to make it work" and you believe your mind and let your conscious mind continue to control your shooting that much more.

You may need a third party to observe this when you play, because your ego mind (conscious mind) will not always tell you the truth. You may think that when you are congratulated that it works and it doesn't affect how well your shoot when the reality of it is you don't shoot as well.

Here is another sad part. (there are lots of sad part here, aren't there? Are you crying yet?) There are some players that when they do get lots of compliments and congratulations they really do play better. And because we see one great player who is able to pick up their game this way, we think that this is the way to get ourselves to play better.

Please, don't believe me in this. Check it out yourself. When you are watching games whether at the pro level or not, take a look at what happens over and over when the game get close. You will see a lot of missing nothing shots for no reason. So many times you will see the

95

person try so much harder and therefore react more and more intensely.

The main point I am trying to make is that it is ever so subtle. The conscious mind just creeps back in and tries to take control again and again when you aren't looking or paying attention.

Have you ever really experienced this difference between trying and letting the "other than conscious mind" and body play? Trust me, if you haven't, try it, it works far better. Maybe not every time, but it feels so good when it does. And sometimes it may even work spectacularly.

So, all of this mental stuff that I am trying to drill (I mean have you put) into your head is to let go of having your conscious mind control your play. Then I want you to let go more of having your conscious mind control your play. And finally, I want you to let go even more of having your conscious mind control your play. Have I mentioned letting go yet? Every concept in these mini lessons and in my book tries to lead you in that direction. That is the purpose of the "Core Principles."

Now that you know this, you just have to keep on practicing letting go. This will be a lifelong process but the results can be remarkable.

But what do you do when you get complimented or someone congratulates you on a great play or shot. You translate it by saying to yourself and doing this. You pat yourself on the back and say," That was a great shot (or play) body. Thank you so much and keep those great shots coming. I know you can do it and I will get out of your way."

When you translate these comments that are made to you, you will have a much better chance of playing even better especially in a tight game or in the final seconds.

Lesson No. 34: Exercises You Must Do to Improve Your Shooting

Here are some exercises for you on how you can begin to implement the ideas I have talked about. When you practice using these exercises you will be allowing your body to learn at a much faster rate. Notice that I have you focusing on one thing at a time.

Doing them one at a time is beneficial so that when you begin to combine them it will be easier. Remember the ideal is to combine focusing on the hook with perfect breathing and relaxation, holding the follow through until the ball reaches the rim, and shooting on the UpForce. The holding of your follow through and shooting on the UpForce will be happening automatically while you are **consciously** focusing on the hook and **consciously** exhaling properly.

Exercise #1

Practice shooting just focusing on your breathing. While working on your breathing, feel your face and see if it is tense or if you have an expression change. When you exhale properly, your face will be very relaxed. To help you with relaxing your face, have a friend observe

97

your face when you shoot. Many times, you won't be aware of what your face is doing. Remember that your exhale is not a blow but a very relaxed sigh which continues until the ball reaches the rim.

Be sure to focus on your breathing when you are doing your fancy moves and when you drive to the basket.

Exercise #2

Practice shooting seeing the ball spinning as it travels to the basket. Make sure you see the ball spinning as it drops through the basket or if it bounces off the rim. You will not be doing this when you shoot in a game. This is just an exercise of awareness.

Exercise #3

Practice shooting with perfect focus on the hook. Ask yourself: Did I **consciously** see the hook the entire time the ball traveled to the basket?

Exercise #4

Practice shooting combining the breathing with staying focused on the hook.

Exercise #5:

Practice shooting observing the trajectory of the ball as it travels to the basket. Make sure you make the arc 6 to 8 feet above the rim.

Exercise #6

Practice shooting letting your arm, wrist and hand come to an absolute stop until your ball reaches the basket. While you are holding your follow through, check it out to make sure your arm, wrist and fingers are very relaxed.

Exercise #7

Practice being aware of whether you are shooting on the UpForce.

Exercise #8

After getting the feel for these first seven exercises, start combining any two of them. Then compiling three with finally working up to combining all five. In case you have forgotten what the five are, they are:

1. **Consciously** focus on the hook
2. Do a relaxed exhale before, as, and after you shoot
3. Holding the finish until the ball reaches the rim
4. Relaxing the arm, wrist, and fingers as you are holding
5. Releasing the ball on the UpForce than

Lesson No. 35: Some Final Thoughts

Here are my final thoughts for you to consider.

Now that you have learned another way of shooting a basketball, you now have to actually work on these concepts. They are not that easy.

99

They are easy to talk about and understand, but they need to be worked on and practiced just like any other skill. The really good news is that although this is a process, the more you work on letting go and focusing properly, the better your shooting will be. Guaranteed!

Reading this through once is just not enough. Please go back to the part on the Core Principles or earlier if you want to and begin again. You will be amazed at how much you will learn the second, third, and fourth time through.

These concepts really need to be experienced in order for you to be able to get the improvement you would like. If you would like some help in actually experiencing these concepts, I can help you cut down on the time it takes for you to learn how to do these things and I can make sure you are really doing them the way they need to be done. So, if you, your team, or any of your friends would like some personal help, please contact me at david@innerbasketball.com and let's figure how to get together in person or on the phone. Call me at 360 305-7084 anytime between 9:00 AM to 9:00 PM Pacific time.

I wish you the very best of luck on your play and I want you to thank your conscious mind for being open to this way of playing and thank your body for being so talented.

And I want to thank you for taking the time and effort to play the mental game. There just isn't a better way to play, is there?

Made in the USA
Charleston, SC
09 April 2013